Paw Prints

Labrador Retrievers

by Jenna Lee Gleisner

Bullfrog Books

Ideas for Parents and Teachers

Bullfrog Books let children practice reading informational text at the earliest reading levels. Repetition, familiar words, and photo labels support early readers.

Before Reading

- Discuss the cover photo. What does it tell them?

- Look at the picture glossary together. Read and discuss the words.

Read the Book

- "Walk" through the book and look at the photos. Let the child ask questions. Point out the photo labels.

- Read the book to the child, or have him or her read independently.

After Reading

- Prompt the child to think more. Ask: Have you ever seen a Labrador retriever? Would you like to play with one?

Bullfrog Books are published by Jump!
5357 Penn Avenue South
Minneapolis, MN 55419
www.jumplibrary.com

Library of Congress Cataloging-in-Publication Data

Names: Gleisner, Jenna Lee, author.
Title: Labrador retrievers / by Jenna Lee Gleisner.
Description: Minneapolis, MN : Jump!, Inc., 2018.
Series: Paw prints
Series: Bullfrog books | Includes index.
Audience: Ages 5 to 8. | Audience: Grades K to 3.
Identifiers: LCCN 2017039656 (print)
LCCN 2017044185 (ebook)
ISBN 9781624967795 (ebook)
ISBN 9781624967788 (hardcover : alk. paper)
Subjects: LCSH: Labrador retriever—Juvenile literature.
Classification: LCC SF429.L3 (ebook)
LCC SF429.L3 G56 2018 (print) | DDC 636.752/7—dc23
LC record available at https://lccn.loc.gov/2017039656

Editor: Kristine Spanier
Book Designer: Molly Ballanger

Photo Credits: Eric Isselee/Shutterstock, cover, 3, 24; Irina oxilixo Danilova/Shutterstock, 1; Capture Light/Shutterstock, 4; RubberBall/SuperStock, 5, 23bl; Kirk Geisler/Shutterstock, 6–7, 23br; Wavebreakmedia/iStock, 8; dezy/Shutterstock, 9; Grigorita Ko/Shutterstock, 10–11, 23tl; Rosa Jay/Shutterstock, 12–13; Anrodphoto/iStock, 14–15; huronphoto/iStock, 16; MintImages/Shutterstock, 17, 23tr; Janet Horton/Alamy, 18–19; THEPALMER/iStock, 20–21; Dora Zett/Shutterstock, 22.

Printed in the United States of America at Corporate Graphics in North Mankato, Minnesota.

Table of Contents

Friendly Hunters

Look! A dog.

What kind?

A Labrador retriever!

What are these
dogs like?

Let's find out!

5

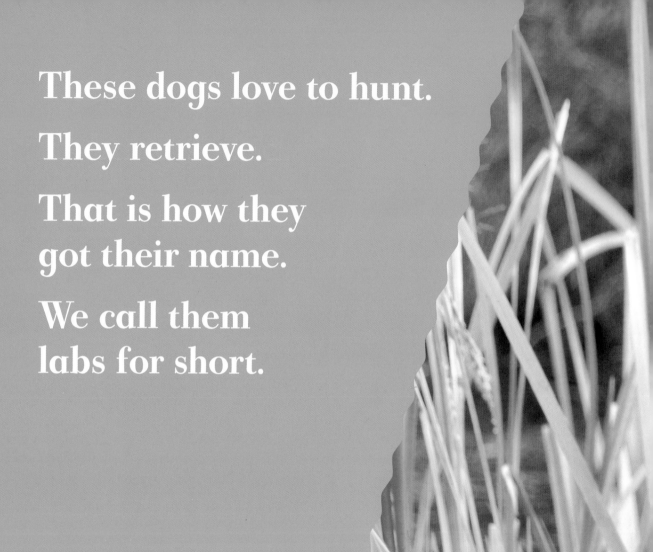

These dogs love to hunt.

They retrieve.

That is how they got their name.

We call them labs for short.

Labs have big bodies.

Strong legs help them run and swim.

Labs have a lot of energy.
They need exercise.

They come in
three colors.

What are they?

Black, yellow,
and chocolate.

fur

Their fur is thick.

It keeps them warm.

Labs listen.

They are friendly.
They make good guide dogs.

Do they love to play?
Yes!

Do you want to play with a lab?

A Labrador Retriever Up Close

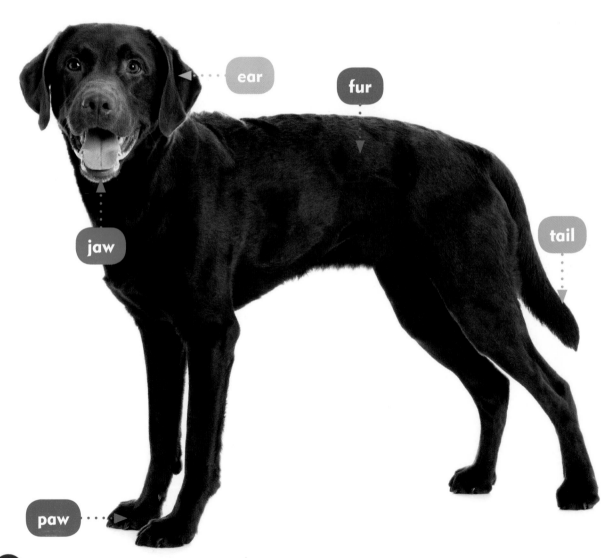

ear

fur

jaw

tail

paw

Picture Glossary

exercise
Physical activity done to stay strong and healthy.

guide dogs
Dogs that are trained to help people.

friendly
Nice and gentle around people.

retrieve
To get something and bring it back.

Index

To Learn More

Learning more is as easy as 1, 2, 3.

1) Go to www.factsurfer.com

2) Enter "labradorretrievers" into the search box.

3) Click the "Surf" button to see a list of websites.

With factsurfer.com, finding more information is just a click away.